The Heartbeat
AFTER THE FOG

THERESA STOVER

ISBN 978-1-0980-4102-1 (paperback)
ISBN 978-1-0980-4316-2 (hardcover)
ISBN 978-1-0980-4103-8 (digital)

Christian Faith Publishing, Inc.
832 Park Avenue
Meadville, PA 16335
www.christianfaithpublishing.com

Printed in the United States of America

To my daughter, Chantal, we went through this together throughout my young adult life and until your young adult life. We've always made a great team and had a strong bond. I love you and feel so blessed to have you as my baby girl, love mom.

CHAPTER 1

Facebook post, June 2, 2014:

> People are saying they can't imagine what I'm going through…Remember when your baby is first born and you stay up all night watching and listening to it breathe? Now imagine staying up all night watching and listening for her to stop breathing. Hardest thing a mom could go through. I am so thankful for all your support.

Cadence passed away two days later.

Her funeral was beautiful and more than I ever pictured in my mind, and trust me, I pictured it many times. I woke up several nights and planned it in my head. Her casket would be lined with pink satin, my good friend would sing "Held" and another would sing "The Cartoon Song" (his son sang the echo, it was the sweetest), and her hair would be beautifully styled and curled by my hairstylist who I had known for so many years. We couldn't get the casket with pink lining, so another friend bought four yards of pink satin to wrap Cadence in and another twist from a brother in Christ as he sang, "He's got the whole world in his hands. He's got the little bitty baby in his hands." That was a beautiful surprise. The Lord and my church family were my biggest and best support. I don't know what I would have done without them—as well as my close family members—and one I never thought would be so close. I'll get to that later.

Cadence was nineteen years old with a tiny frame, long brown hair, and a unique personality. She was diagnosed with cerebral palsy when she was only ten months old. The doctor noticed she was not growing well and not meeting average milestones of other children. With a speech impediment, she took some time to get her words out with having to take a breath every couple of words, but she loved to talk to others—when they had the patience to allow her to finish a sentence. I will never forget our conversations up until her death. I would lie in the bed next to her and talk about so many things.

Since Cadence's passing, I have met several people that have lost their children, especially as a licensed mental health counselor. One question that has been asked to me is, "What's worse, losing a child with warning or losing a child with no warning?" I don't have an answer for that. Both are difficult. I just know my experience.

Many people have shared their story with both, knowing they were going to pass or a fast death from an accident. I didn't realize how many people have children pass away until mine, some from an illness, car accident, drug overdose, drunk driving, or other tragic events—slow death, fast death, both hurt and both need to be mourned. We all mourn in different ways. Some parents want to be left alone, some dig into work or other tasks to escape their feelings, some sleep most of the day, some tell jokes to cover the pain, and some are able to go through the stages of grief at a faster rate: denial, anger, bargaining, depression, and acceptance. I feel as if I was able to go through these while Cadence was weakening; maybe that is an advantage of knowing. I knew it was time for her to go, but it still hurt.

I dug into my college work. When Cadence was sick, I focused on a master's degree in mental health counseling and then quickly began a PhD program in clinical Christian counseling. I realize now that I was escaping my emotions by jumping from one task to another. In a way, I think I knew. I thought as long as I feel this way, I might as well accomplish my goals. I didn't realize it was affecting others until I started my internship on an inpatient unit. Without realizing my lack of emotion, I was told that I did not express anything on my face and I focused only on the job at hand. I didn't socialize or get involved with other coworkers which is not good when on a clinical team. I quickly started to become aware of how I came across to others. Nothing changed though; I didn't know how to change. How do

I make myself feel when there is no emotion? Or are there so many emotions that it becomes overwhelming? It's just easier not to feel.

*****

I knew Cadence was dying. I could see it, feel it. I knew her like no one else ever could, except God. When she was sixteen, I began to notice she couldn't remember important information and people. I thought I was just confused at first. Then her teacher from her class called and told me Cadence was sleeping a lot in school and had to be reminded of her friends' names in the room. This meant it was real. No more feeling it was in my imagination.

I called the doctor right away and they followed up with some tests. Since she had already been experiencing grand mal seizures since age five, we wanted to test this area first.

That was a frightening time, her first seizure at five years old. She was convulsing until she stopped and then nothing. This went on for about an hour and a half until rescue finally got to my house and stopped it all. We found out at that time that seizures affect the memory. After most of Cadence's grand mal seizures, she would forget simple things, such as friends or family names, for about three to four months. The grand mal seizures happened about four times per year, usually when she was too hot with fever or was outside. So we tried to keep her in the air condition as much as possible. I was not surprised the medical team wanted to check this area first; it made sense.

Cadence spent three days in the hospital with electroencephalogram (EEG) probes on her head and with me by her side. There are about eleven probes all over her head, and then her head was wrapped in bandage to hold them all in place. We made the best of this time with talking, laughing, and reading books. All seemed well; she was alert and happy. When the tech came in the room to take off the equipment from her head, I told them they would not find anything. She was alert, talking, and laughing the whole time. A little later in the day, the neurologist came in to speak with us. I was confident the test did not show anything or any irregularities. I was quickly and painfully proven wrong.

The EEG not only showed Cadence was having seizures, but she was having them every thirty seconds. And she was having several types of petite seizures. The doctor called it Lennox-Gastaut syndrome, a severe form of epilepsy found in children. I began to notice after this diagnosis and lots of research to educate as to what to look for in Cadence's behaviors. I noticed when she would stare straight up for a couple seconds or one hand would shake back and forth or one foot would shake back and forth as well as other signs that a seizure was happening in the moment. Seizures cause individuals to sleep a lot which fit the fact that Cadence was sleeping every day at school and wanted to go to bed at six thirty at night due to feeling so tired. This fit her symptoms for sure. After a typical grand mal seizure, Cadence would sleep from six to eight hours and her memory might take from just a few days and up to four months, so I can imagine why she would want to sleep a lot during the day now.

Along with a seizure disorder, Cadence had another medical condition while growing up, which we thought was severe constipation. She was hospitalized several times in her life due to obstructions, excessive vomiting, and constipation. Little did I know then that when bacteria could sit in the bowels for too long, the gases move into the organs and cause them to weaken. It was just a matter of time before her organs could be too weak to function properly. I just didn't know when or how badly they could deteriorate.

With Cadence having two severe and chronic medical conditions, every time she was hospitalized, I wondered if this was the time. I would picture different situations that I would find her or how it would happen. That's enough to keep a mom awake at night, wondering, praying, crying.

Chapter 2

I remember when Cadence was born, she was fourteen weeks early. Yes, she was born at twenty-six weeks! She experienced some head trauma, there was bleeding on her brain, and she was so tiny. Young and naive, I thought all she needed was to grow and become stronger. I had no idea of the effects on the brain and struggles of a preemie baby. She was the most beautiful baby.

When she was still in the hospital, growing and getting stronger, I visited a friend's church where we prayed for Cadence. During the music worship, they sang "He's got the little bitty baby in his hands." That's when I knew he was with her. And this was the reason for my loving, wonderful surprise at her funeral.

Ten months later, Cadence was diagnosed with cerebral palsy. I was in a fog. A team of medical personnel were all talking at the same time, saying all this medical mumble jumble that I couldn't understand and throwing out the initials CP. Finally, I asked them to stop talking as if I was not in the room and fill me in on what they are saying. As they told me about my tiny baby never having the ability of making the same milestones of other children, the fog got bigger. Was I in a dream? I couldn't believe what they were saying. In fact, I didn't believe what they were saying at first—all my baby needed was to grow and get stronger. The fog lasted a few weeks, maybe longer. I prayed to God that Cadence would be able to talk. I wanted her to be able to tell me her needs and also she would be able to tell me if anyone was ever trying to harm her.

Cadence never walked, but *goodness*, she sure did talk. *Haha!* This little girl knew how to get her needs met, and what she wanted, she wanted *now*! She had a wonderful memory when she was younger. That's why we were so shocked when she couldn't remember her friends' names. She was a loving, sweet child and touched lives of anyone she came into contact.

People couldn't help but be drawn to such an amazing little girl. She started talking at age five with her first words being "Iwuvoooh." Oh my gosh! I cried and called several people to let them know Cadence said, "I love you." What a sweet girl! I knew she would talk eventually. I prayed that she would and she did. Soon after, she talked more and more—a lot. *Haha!*

She called for me the most, "Mama." "Mama…Mama…Mama." So much that when I answered, she would just stare at me. I realized that she really just wanted to know I was there and that she was the most important in the room, which she undoubtedly was. *LOL!*

Sometimes when she would call me, I would answer, "Yes, dear"—no answer.

She would call again, "Mama."

"Yes, dear"—no answer.

After about five times of her calling, "Mama," I would reply saying, "Cadence, you better have something to say this time."

Cadence would then reply with "Your hair…is pretty" or "I like…your shoes."

I couldn't help but laugh. She would get me every time.

As a teenager, she had crushes on boys. I remember she had a crush on a guy at church. She would look at him in awe. When the girlfriend of this guy went up to him to talk, Cadence would give a dirty look and say *Grrr* with a mean face. If we talked to Cadence about him, she would smile and her face would light up. She really liked this guy. His girlfriend didn't mind; she understood. They were both at her funeral. He cried throughout.

Cadence started tap dancing a few years before she got sick. She had difficulty using her legs, so she would dance in a gait trainer. This is where she stands in a metal brace; it holds her up by supporting her waist with Velcro, and she could walk in it—or dance. Her face would light up with happiness and achievement.

So many memories…

*****

With her favorite word being "Mama," she would say it probably one hundred times a day. That's the first thing I missed when she passed away. I've heard that when someone is alive, the most trying things they would do or say are what you miss the most. Not that I didn't like her to call me, but so many times in a day—good grief. LOL! One way we like to keep her memory alive in my house now is the kids will say it over and over again, "Mama…Mama…Mama… Mama, who am I?" *Haha!*

Then we laugh with joy and fond memories. The kids purposely act out like her or make other comments like her and smile. Oh, we love to keep her memory alive.

*****

During therapy, I tell my clients who have lost a child to do whatever it takes to remember, laugh, tell stories, and go out to their favorite place for dinner on their child's birthday.

We celebrate and remember Cadence in my home as much as possible. We don't make it a grieving session by any means. Cadence loved it when we laughed and was upset when we cried. Mostly for her birthday or the anniversary of her death, we all get together— whoever wants to join—and I always invite all her friends on social media too. Usually, a group of us get together: me, my husband, our children, and my ex-husband (Cadence's dad) and his wife. We come up with something that Cadence loved, such as ice cream, pizza, or Chinese food.

One year, we all gathered at my house with several different flavors of ice cream and all the toppings. Friends and family joined in on social media, sharing photos of eating ice cream in memory of Cadence. One year, a whole group of us met at Cadence's favorite pizza place. If someone wasn't able to meet with us, they ate pizza at home. We tell stories, eat, and even tell of our struggles with missing her. It's like a one big support group of many people that love Cadence so much. We are able to learn and grow together as we move forward in our lives without Cadence.

I feel like many people who have lost their children feel they can't talk about their dear child, whether it's because they don't want to "bring down the room" or worry they may "feel" and don't want to have or show emotion. They want to act as if they are okay and moving forward. This is because society moves forward so quickly and leaves you back thinking, *What just happened? How can everyone move on so quickly? Why am I not moving forward?* Yes, I go through my time of grieving. Usually it's alone in my car as I talk to God about her. I just want my heart to beat again.

I found that he is the only one who truly knows my heart and can comfort me in the moment. The main thing is he doesn't throw out clichés or Bible verses. He listens with no interruptions. I could feel his comfort in the moment. It's okay to feel emotions and to sit with those feelings. Never allow anyone or yourself to tell you anything differently. Never allow anyone to tell you it's been enough time and you need to move on. Always remember God is with you and you are never alone in your grief.

If we don't remember our children and talk about them, what was their reason for being here to begin with? I don't ever want to say, "Remember that little girl I had that one time?" I want to always remember her. Not in an unhealthy way but in a "she did exist" and was my daughter for nineteen years.

I no longer mourn daily and with time, that gets less and less. When I do, I talk to God, usually in my car, and tell him how I am feeling.

CHAPTER 3

The first year is the most difficult with firsts of all events. Their birthday, Christmas, Thanksgiving, mother's or father's day, and so on. I learned the second year that I was depressed from the time Cadence was hospitalized in April through her funeral on June 7. This was brought to my attention by coworkers. I was again told that I had no emotion or expression on my face and was only focused at the task on hand.

After this reality, I was able to keep track of this time, and sure enough, the third year was the same beginning in April and ending on June 7. Now that I am aware, I know it's going to happen. My loving friends, coworkers, and family know it's going to happen and it's okay. I allow myself to mourn in this time and let myself off the hook for having sad days. I know it won't last. The fourth year seemed the same as the last three. This year though, the fifth year, I noticed less sad days than in the previous years. I was told by friends that they also noticed a difference in me this year. They said they were looking for it in support but didn't notice the same affect. I love my friends/coworkers for noticing and being such great friends.

*****

I have heard though from people who have lost their children many years ago that they go through emotions at different times and different years. One lost her two-year-old twins in a car accident. She shared that she feels depressed at different times in her life or milestones of her children, such as she mourned for months because of their twentieth birthday—eighteen years after their death.

We all mourn differently and at different times throughout our lives and that's okay. If we need to seek counseling at different stages, that's okay too.

People like to say, "Give it to God." That's supposed to make it all go away. That's not what I mean at all when I say I go to God with my feelings. I just talk to him aloud and feel comfort. There's a difference. I don't "give it to him." I still feel the emotions.

I'm not afraid to remind others that I may experience some emotions at times. I have feelings and that's okay. I'm not going to ignore the fact that I had a child and now she's gone. It's always okay to seek help if needed.

CHAPTER 4

Sometimes I allow myself to go back and remember Cadence's last couple of years.

After she got a G-tube put in, she felt sick a lot. Her intestines didn't seem to be working and she was throwing up more times than not. The doctors kept telling me to give her stool softeners and medication to help the intestines contract and work on their own, but as was always the case, it just didn't ever seem to help. Now she's on a liquid diet and it still can't seem to pass through her intestines with ease. She was a little over seventeen by now when we found out that she was unable to swallow food by mouth. Everything, especially liquid, would go straight into her lungs. The G-tube would go into her stomach with bypassing the mouth and throat. The doctor put a hole in her stomach, and the liquid food would be pumped from a machine much like the one used for dosing IV fluid through the G-tube and into her stomach. With this, there's still the issue of intestines not contracting. I thought, *It's liquid. How much do her intestines still need to do?*

This was a difficult time for Cadence though as she loved food so much and now, she couldn't eat any—no more pizza or ice cream. Well, on Thanksgiving, I gave her a bit of cool whip. That's another memory we share on that holiday. We have a scoop of cool whip for Cadence.

She began being hospitalized more and more after the G-tube was inserted. I could sense her body getting weaker and weaker. Shortly after, I put another bed in her room for the nights I needed to stay in and wait for her to be sick. This is when I started planning her funeral more and more in my mind. I knew it was coming. I would pray and pray for God to show me when and where. I would pray that he would end her suffering and stop all the pain, sickness, and hospital needlesticks. I knew by this time he was not going to heal her here on Earth but that her healing would be in heaven.

From eighteen to nineteen years old, Cadence spent more time in the hospital than out. In April 2014, she was hospitalized weekly. Then at the end of May, she was hospitalized just hours after being released on the same day. She had very little memory of family or friends. Cadence and I both knew it was time. We spent most of our time talking about heaven, family in heaven, and any fear or concerns she may feel.

The doctor came in the hospital room to have a somber, heartfelt talk with me about the fact that Cadence's organs are weak and ready to shut down. She said it was time to consider hospice. I called my ex-husband as he was in and out visiting and staying with Cadence as she spent this time in the hospital. I asked him to come back to the hospital as we had a choice to make. As I waited for Cadence's dad to get to the hospital, I asked for a second opinion from another doctor to be certain that hospice was the next and final step.

I called my pastor by now and asked him to come pray for Cadence and for the hardest choice of our life. My pastor was also waiting for my call to give an update on the progress or lack of progress. We talked earlier that morning and he asked me to keep him informed. With the help of my pastor and prayer, we filled Cadence's dad in of the news of hospice, weakening organs, and the second opinion who agreed with the first. Both doctors agree that it is time and that Cadence was not going to live for more than a couple of weeks.

With all agreeing it was time for hospice, the hospital called for transport. Again, the fog—was this really happening? Was this real? The doctors took out the ventilator as Cadence was in and out of consciousness. Her little body had enough. She was ready.

As rescue put Cadence on the stretcher at the hospital to move location, red cross called my cell phone with an urgent call from my oldest daughter, a marine. She was on deployment overseas and got the message that Cadence was in the hospital again and it was time to get an emergency flight home. I filled her in on all that was happening and the choice for hospice. She asked how long she had to get home or to ask for the flight. I looked at the doctor, and she replied, "Now."

*****

It took three days for Cadence's big sister to get home. I remember meeting her at the airport with my ex-husband as we all dropped to our knees and wept when we saw one another. The emotions were too intense. We hadn't seen her for months and our other daughter was about to pass away. It was just too much.

Cadence spent six days in the hospice. The doctor said two weeks, but I knew better. I could feel it. Family and friends from all over came to see Cadence. There were friends from school, family from out of town, friends who came to see her in the neonatal intensive care unit when she was born, her first babysitter, neighbors throughout Cadence's life, and others from various areas. We laughed, cried, and talked about everything and anything. I spent time lying in bed with Cadence, talking about God and heaven. We had discussions about her being ready and that I will see her again one day.

She went into the hospice on a Thursday; the weekend came and went faster than I would have liked. Family called to say when they were coming to see her. Some would say they will be there Wednesday to see her and say goodbye. I remember telling them that would be too late. I remember telling friends that it was going to happen on Wednesday, and they would chuckle and say, "You and your Wednesday." I can't explain why, but I could just feel it.

Throughout our time at the hospice, my ex-husband and his wife and I spent most of our time there, along with Cadence's big sister. My husband spent most of his time at home with our younger children, trying to keep their lives as normal as possible. At the time, they were only seven and nine years old. They came to visit one time in the hospice as my son read to her in bed as he did so many times before. Cadence loved for him to read to her, and the memory for my son is an important one. Outside of that, the kids spent the rest of the time doing their normal everyday activities. My husband made the comment many times that he wished my mother would have been there to help with the kids so he could have spent more time with Cadence and supporting me since my mother didn't want to be there to do it.

I called my mother when Cadence went into hospice and she told me she was going out of town on a trip. I reminded her of what was happening with my daughter, her granddaughter. She left anyway and was not there when Cadence passed.

I believe the Lord had all this planned out already and all happened as it was supposed to happen.

Sometimes, I felt as if I were watching all of this happening as if it were a dream—as if I were up above watching, watching people come in and out of the room, listening to everyone saying goodbye, watching everything happening like puzzle pieces going into place, like all that happened in her life led up to this day, at this time. I became aware of Cadence's purpose in this life and the people she touched along the way. I became aware that Cadence was never "mine." She was a gift from God that I was blessed to have in my life, love, and guide to anywhere she was supposed to go to make a difference in this world.

CHAPTER 5

Up until now, I didn't have a very good relationship with my ex's wife. In fact, prior to this, I didn't respect her for several reasons, reasons that really didn't seem to matter anymore as we spent our time at the hospice. She wanted to be part of all that was happening and I felt the Lord lying on my heart to allow that to happen.

The doctor called me over when we first got to the hospice to tell us how long he felt she had to live. My ex-husband's wife looked at me and motioned as if asking permission to join the conversation. At that time, I felt a lift of any ailment I felt. It was gone. I motioned back to her, wanting her to join in the conversation, and I was glad I did. A couple of days later, her mom joined—another I didn't care for and knew she didn't care for me. This would become someone else that my heart was no longer cold; none of the past actions or emotions mattered anymore. All the worldly issues and bitterness over little things just don't matter once a tragic event such as this happens.

My support at this time was my husband; my ex-husband, his wife, and her mom; my oldest daughter; and several church members and friends. I am truly grateful for them all.

*****

We all met with the funeral home director on Monday. It was me and my husband and ex-husband and his wife. I told the funeral director what I had planned out in my mind so he could create it just as I pictured for so many nights. When he said he couldn't get the pink satin, I cried. I wanted what I created in my mind for my precious little girl. Pink was Cadence's favorite color and satin was just so soft for her little body to be placed in the coffin. My ex-husband's wife knew how important the details were for the funeral and stated that she would make this happen and that she would help make the funeral as I picture. She was so kind and caring and I was grateful she was there. Something I never would have thought in my wildest dreams prior to this happening.

*****

Tuesday, Cadence was in and out of consciousness as people filtered in and out to say their last goodbyes. Cadence cried on and off throughout the day as we all did. A friend from Cadence's school came to play his keyboard and sing a song from her favorite singer. That made the whole room cry, hold one another, and hold Cadence. People loved her. I loved her.

I remember I would lay awake in the bed next to Cadence and watch her breathe; that's when I sent that post—I was literally waiting for my little girl to take her last breath. It was about 6:00 a.m. on Wednesday when Nurse Bob came in the room. He asked how long she had been breathing like she was—it sounded different or forced like she was back on the ventilator only there was not a ventilator. My oldest daughter and their cousin left the room at that time as they spent that last night with Cadence too.

I told Nurse Bob that her breathing started to sound that way a couple of hours ago. He said, "Call her dad. It's time." *It's time...It's time*, the words wouldn't leave my head. *It's time.* I felt panicky and foggy as if I was not ready for the words, "It's time." I felt like I kept moving throughout the room but not really going anywhere. *It's time.*

I called Cadence's dad and said to him, "It's time." I called family members waiting for the call, "It's time." The words just kept going on over and over in my head and aloud to others. I couldn't stand still. It was as if I didn't know what that meant. I remember asking another nurse, "What does that mean, 'It's time'?" She just stared at me as if I were crazy. I'm sure I wasn't making any sense.

I lied in the bed next to Cadence and told her that her dad was on his way as she appeared unconscious by now, eyes closed and no verbal response. I said, "Please wait for him and when he says, 'Peace out, Buttercup,' you run, run fast and know I will see you again and I love you so much."

For years, every time Cadence and her dad would spend some time together, they would leave one another with, "Peace out," and his nickname for her was Buttercup, so saying this just fit.

Cadence's dad got to the hospice about 6:55 a.m. He knelt down next to her on the bed. I don't know what they talked about as it was their moment. They spoke for some time and as soon as Cadence's dad said, "Peace out, Buttercup," Cadence took her last breath. This was a long gasp as if all the air was leaving her body, a sound that I will never, ever forget. As Cadence took her last breath, my ex-husband's wife grabbed me and held me as I wept. That's a bond that will never be broken. It is molded in my heart forever.

Cadence passed on a Wednesday at 7:15 a.m.

*****

I sat with Cadence while we waited for the funeral director. Friends came to support me instead of going to work for the day. My pastor stayed the whole time for prayer and support. My husband came too. The kids were told their sister passed that morning. My oldest daughter felt alone as she spent time with family coming to join together. This was so difficult as she came home from deployment just in time to watch her sister pass and then went back only ten days later. This is something we continue to work on and heal from today.

As I watched the funeral director wheel Cadence's covered body out to the building, it was like being in a dream.

Once Cadence was out of the building, I left the hospice for the last time. I felt so tired, weak, and drained and didn't want to drive home alone. I called my big brother who lived three hours away to talk with on the way home from the hospice building. As I drove up my driveway, I noticed he was parked on the side of the house. He said he came as soon as he got the call that morning, "It is time." He held me as I cried, again.

CHAPTER 6

As mentioned in the beginning of this book, the funeral was absolutely beautiful with all the seats filled and people standing all around in the church. Cadence's dad is in the Army National Guard, so it seemed his entire troupe attended—of course, friends and family all in pink in memory of Cadence's favorite color. Guys wore pink shirts and pink ties. At one point, I stood up and scanned the sanctuary—again in the fog or dream mode—looking at all the people Cadence touched in her life here. That didn't even include all the people that could not attend.

I couldn't believe this was happening, all the pieces of the puzzle being put together. It was almost complete.

The viewing was first; I didn't know my part. Am I supposed to stand next to the casket as I've seen others do at funerals? Do I walk around and listen to how other people feel about my daughter passing away? Do I allow others to walk up to me to say how sorry they are for my loss? What does a mom do at her own child's funeral? The fog had already set in. I'm in "this is a dream" mode. I talked to some people, and I watched as people talked with Cadence in the casket. My beautician fixed and curled Cadence's long hair. Cadence was wrapped in pink satin. It was, again, more than I had pictured.

The pastor, who knew Cadence for many years by this time, knew exactly what to say about her. The songs were just beautiful and I love my friends for singing them. The song the music pastor and his friend sang, "He's got the little bitty baby in his hands," was an unexpected gift. All the songs were amazing. The first one, "Held," caused people to cry. The second, "The cartoon song," allowed people to laugh. There is no way to explain the emotions of this funeral.

After the pastor completed and all the songs were sung, my mother stood up with a dozen pink roses. She handed one to each family member and we walked up in a line. Each of us placed a pink rose in the casket.

I watched as the funeral instructor closed the casket, rolled my little girl's body out of the church, and drove her away.

And it was done.

CHAPTER 7

Cadence's big sister went back on deployment—back to reality but still not completely grasping what just happened to her sister, the sister with whom she spent her whole childhood, had slumber parties, and shared her life.

I went back to work after being off for three weeks. I was ready to get back to reality and see my coworkers and clients. I knew I might have some struggle with life for a while. The best part of being a mental health counselor though is we have an entire hallway full of therapists. They were all supportive, most attended the funeral.

I went to a therapist for loss a couple of weeks after Cadence passed. She talked about the loss of her husband and the loss of her clients' loved ones. We talked nothing about my experience, my feelings, or where I was in my process of mourning. I left more depressed than when I arrived because I just wanted to be heard. I wasn't going to go back, but my supervisor at the time encouraged me to go back and tell this therapist how I felt. So I went back the following week and told her how I felt at the last session. The therapist admitted that the session should not have gone that way and she was sorry for the way I felt. Then she proceeded to go on about this happening to her sister before and how her sister felt. I got up and walked out and told her I would not be back.

This experience with my therapist gave me a great insight into the therapist I want to be regarding helping others who have lost a child. I will never know "exactly" how anyone feels—that's the Lord's area of expertise; he knows their heart. I can relate though and I can listen. They can be heard.

When a parent is going through such a loss as a child, people are so loving and want to say supportive verbiage but tend to say a lot of clichés and Bible verses. This is loving but not helpful in the time of mourning. I wanted someone to listen or maybe even try to understand what I was going through. I truly love my friends and supportive people in my life and will always remember how they were there for me when I needed them. I love them so much!

One friend told me, "I know *exactly* how you feel. My daughter moved to North Carolina and I don't get to see her." Really!? You know *exactly* how I feel? Is your child still alive? Sometimes, if you don't know what to say, it's more helpful to not say anything at all.

I had taken a term off from working on my PhD as soon as Cadence began being hospitalized in May, and now I was ready to not only go back to work but to continue in my studies. The first course I was scheduled to go back to was called "Joy in the Midst of Mourning." This was fitting. I began reading my new course in college and realized the Lord is my strength. He knows my heart and exactly where I am in my process of mourning. He will listen with no interruption. And he comforts me when I am alone. I still look to him for comfort when I am feeling the loss of Cadence. The times a year or special events when I miss her terribly, he is there.

I remember still being in a fog after two and a half months. I missed Cadence so much! I needed to remember her, cry over her, and let some emotions go. So one Sunday, I told the family to all go to church as I would stay home. I took out Cadence's scrapbooks; took out picture after picture, remembering the times of the picture; cried; and mourned my loss. This went on for three hours. After I had gone through every picture, I felt so lifted and lighter.

I feel like when we have a great, heavy loss as this, it's as if we are wearing a heavy armor. We wear this day in and day out. We wear it to work, church, social events, the grocery store, everywhere we go. Sometimes, we are able to take off the armor once we get home and crawl into bed. After my three hours of grieving this Sunday though, all the armor had been lifted. I was so much lighter, and it did not return.

I was able to finally, really move forward. I am not afraid to talk about Cadence or celebrate her. I can talk about her and smile or laugh. I love my family to talk about her too and share memories. Her memory stays alive in my house.

*****

I feel as if everyone who comes into my office for counseling is meant to be there. God doesn't make mistakes. I have had so many people come see me about the loss of their child, even without knowing I have also lost a child. Then when they say, "No one knows how I feel," I can honestly and lovingly say, "I do know. Please tell me about your loss." Together we come up with ways to cope, mourn, process, and remember their precious child.

CHAPTER 8

After losing one child, some of us focus more on keeping our other children healthy. I couldn't bear the thought of losing another child. I realize my kids are not "mine." I learned that with the death of Cadence. They will pass when it's their time and I have no control. I love them so much though and I will protect them until the end.

I have an eleven-year-old daughter, also a preemie like Cadence. This child was born at twenty-eight weeks. Cadence had a lot more issues with having seizures, cerebral palsy, and being born at twenty-six weeks. I begged the Lord the night my younger preemie baby was born to not allow the same issues and struggles. I remember crying all night, begging, and praying to God. I thought all was well until…

A year ago, she was only ten at the time, my daughter was hospitalized. She had problems her whole life with her intestines, feeling bloated, encopresis, and began throwing up. She was never thoroughly potty trained in this area and I didn't know the cause. I'm not sure why it didn't come up in my mind prior to the hospitalization, but we found out that her intestines were not working; they were not contracting. In this moment it hit me—this is the same as Cadence's.

My daughter went through depression due to connecting the fact that Cadence had this too. She asked me in the kitchen one night, "Mom, did Cadence have this too and is it why she died?" I replied that Cadence had more issues with having seizures, but she did also have this and now that we know what is happening, we are better able to make sure she is healthy and lives a long happy life. She said that is wasn't fair that the Lord took Cadence. I stated none of this is fair and we talked about how much I have learned from Cadence having the same thing. We talked about the fact that if it weren't for Cadence, we wouldn't know any of this; we wouldn't know what research to find or to try new medical practices. Who else has a big sister in heaven taking care of her little sister on Earth? Cadence is truly a blessing.

Don't get me wrong. I wish I would have researched all of this when Cadence was alive. I do have guilt. I truly didn't know. I mean, I knew she had issues with her intestines. I did what the doctor told me: "give her stool softeners" and meds to help the intestines contract. I didn't know.

This time, now that I do know, I had tests run to find out why my daughter's intestines didn't contract, mostly self-pay so no one could tell me no or come up with other reasons she was having these symptoms. We found that she had a trauma at birth, also a preemie and also a natural birth (should have been a C-section which was planned but didn't happen). A vertebra in her neck was turned out of place which had exposed the nerve to the intestines, the vagus nerve. The body created a cartilage to protect that nerve. When the cartilage was created, it began to pinch the nerve, causing it to be blocked from doing its job in the intestines.

We had her organs tested in worry that they were weakening such as Cadence's weakened. We found this was the case. She went into detox to clean out her organs as toxins had gone through her body. She was only allowed minimal foods that her body would accept without feeling sick. She was sick a lot after being hospitalized and missed a lot of school. Most food made her sick and her stomach would bloat easily. Eventually, the school put her on hospital homebound due to missing so much school. She was on at least six different medications, twice a day.

With help from prayer, family, and friends, we were able to find a doctor to help with her vertebrae. This doctor heard of my daughter through a coworker and friend of mine and was eager to see if he could help. He used a tool on my daughter's neck where a vertebra is out of place and moved it away to release the vagus nerve. After the procedure, she has to lay down for twenty to forty minutes and no strenuous activity for three days. He said if it works, she will feel as if she needs to use the bathroom soon. That was when my daughter realized we "feel" in this area.

She was lying as she was instructed when she asked, "Mom, I have to ask you something, but it's really embarrassing."

I replied, "What, honey?"

She said, "What am I supposed to feel?" She was able to answer that question for herself very quickly.

This procedure worked the first time! She knew quickly what she was supposed to "feel" and now she was able to do so. Her intestines were working! The only feeling she ever felt before was the pain of the enlarged BM that may pass one time per month and cause horrible cramping and bloating. Now, it was normal and every day. The only problem now is this procedure needs to be done several times per month.

Now, it's been a year and we recently got the good news that her organs have healed entirely. She can begin adding more choices of food in her diet at little amounts at a time.

We are looking into surgery to fix the cartilage permanently. We are hopeful and thankful for all we have learned to keep our daughter, this little girl, here longer.

We are so blessed to have had Cadence in our lives for the time we had her here and that she continues to be with us.

About the Author

Theresa Stover is a licensed mental health counselor and now helps others in grief and healing. She has extensive training in trauma treatment and is nationally certified in trauma-focused cognitive behavioral therapy. Theresa works part-time at a private practice as well as part-time at a community-based treatment center focusing on trauma, depression, and other life experiences.